CHESTER CITY WALLS

Chester City Walls: A Poet's Mosaic
Published by Poetry Space Ltd. 2015

This edition first published in Great Britain in 2015
by Poetry Space Ltd.
Poetry Space Ltd. Company No. 7144469
21 Davis Close, Barrs Court, Bristol, BS30 7BU

Printed and Bound in Great Britain
By Poetry Space Ltd
www.poetryspace.co.uk

ISBN : 978-1-909404-23-6

CHESTER CITY WALLS

A POET'S MOSAIC

Julia D. McGuinness

Chester City Walls

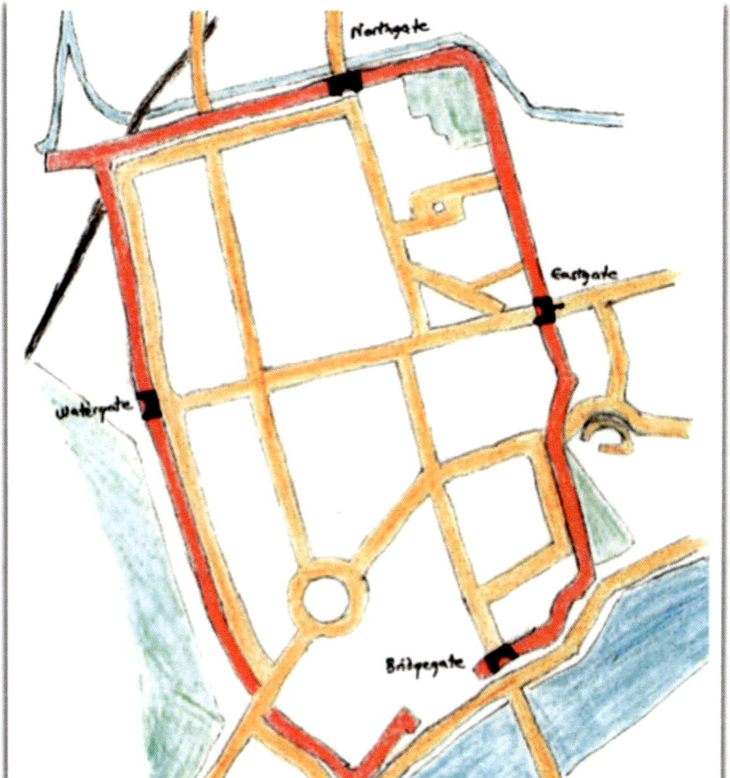

Prelude

Chester City

Walled city: playing-card compact,
defined by ranks of Roman spades,
ramparting turf and timber lines
till Empire's eagle fluttered, fled.

Here, Charles watched his Royalists lose
heart in battle on the baize plain.
Queen's faces too have graced the pack –
Aethelflaeda, Victoria.

Scuffed and dog-eared sandstone edges
once patrolled, now promenaded.
Tourists, traders, shoppers, buskers'
coins clink; jewellers' trays glint diamond.

Resting square in England's green palm:
Field and forest etched by Welsh hills,
face-up till dark turns out clubs, pubs:
"I wouldn't walk the walls at night."

Part 1: Northgate to Eastgate

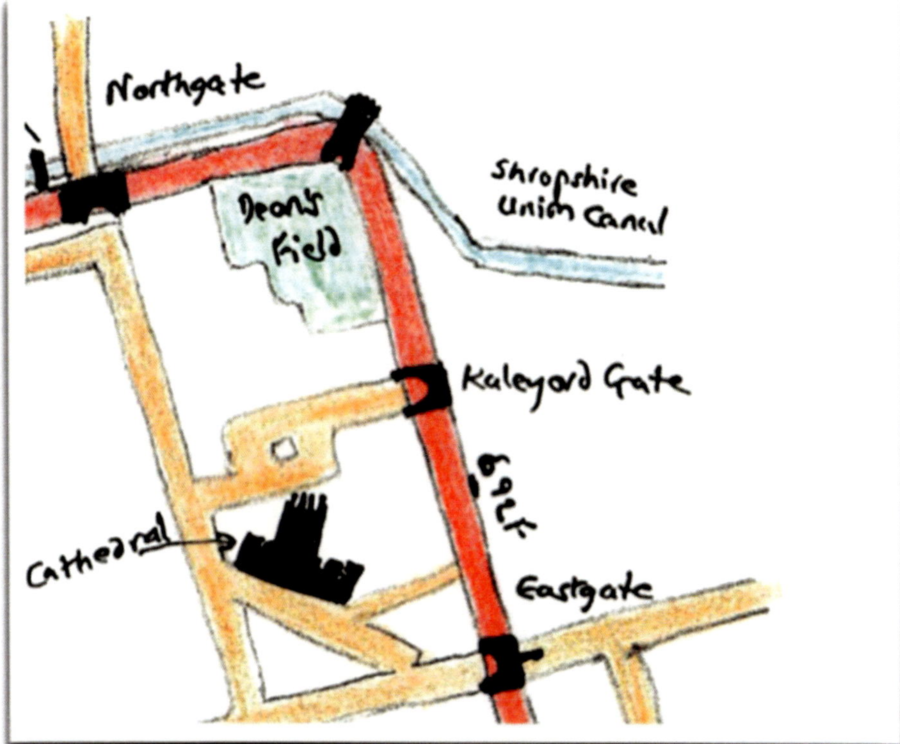
Northgate
Shropshire Union Canal
Dean's Field
Kaleyard Gate
Cathedral
Eastgate

North Facing

'the most elevated section of the walls; the most spectacular and evocative.'

Seagulls speed on the breeze,
swoop the canal, plunge
and snatch the ducks' scraps
to a convulsion of quacks.
Height endows mastery.

Is this why men build walls,
quarrying rock, laying
line upon line, sandstone
abutment crowned
with an artefact prouder still?

At Northgate's edge, Wall
soars sheer in a shiver of air.
A jogger brushes by, nudges
my body to pulse at the parapet
and my breath gasps, what if?

Traversings: From Patrol…

That hard winter of '81 it was 'the North
face of the Eiger' for masons mounted
up this stretch of Wall. I walk taut,
steady my hands on uneven coping,
stare the sharp plunge down to canal.

Enemies climb Walls to cross
and seize the oystered within.
Defenders tread the shell's rim
as I do now, eyes on edge.
The drop has turned me watchman.

The air, ghosted with cold threats;
my steps, a solid pendulum throb;
lamp-posts, spining the way
like sentries to mark the line
in circled light at fringe of dark.

Phoenix Tower bulks as Wall
elbows round to frame a field.
I blink before such open green
regenerating city's breath,
as Roman barracks sleep beneath.

Walls by Numbers

In the 70's AD, the Romans founded Chester as a fortress, Deva Victrix. It was 20% larger than other fortresses they built in Britannia.

The Amphitheatre was built in the 1st century, with seats for 7,000 spectators.

The Walls circuit is around 2 miles long.

The Water Tower and spur wall were built by John de Helpeston in 1322 for a fee of £100. The spur wall up to Bonewaldesthorne's Tower is over 30 metres long.

After the Civil War there were only 6,000 civilians left in Chester.

A rare hoard of 122 Anglo-Saxon coins was found near Pemberton's Parlour in 1914.

In 1997, Chester hosted the European Walled Towns Symposium.

In 1799, the charge or 'murage' for crossing the Walls for a loaded wagon was eightpence (8d) if leaving the city, 4d if coming in.

By 1700, Chester's population was probably approaching 8,000, placing it in a second rank of some 25 English towns with 5,000 or more inhabitants.

Kaleyard Gate was constructed in 1275 to give the Benedictine monks easier access to their vegetable gardens. Chester Cathedral keeps its curfew, locking the gate at 9pm each night.

Repair work in 1883 unearthed over 200 complete or part pieces of Roman tombstones in the north Wall, presumably used as filler-material in 3rd Century repairs. They are now in the City's Grosvenor Museum.

Noli Me Tangere

They had forgotten the gentleness
of hands, how fingers could soothe eyes,
warm limbs, linger in folds of joints,
trace round bodies, stroke letter-lines
as strange tongues softly stumbled
over their messages in hushed respect.
It was not always so, once

they were pounded out of home,
held down, hammered and split.
Slower hands healed their trauma,
gifted shape and colour with kinder tools.
They learned their value in aurei
and tears; found standing in the world,
held the identity of their dead, till

the desperate wrench of urgent hands,
war-calloused, forced them out,
reckless of a nose's contour,
hooves, spears or dates. They broke
shoulders in a fearful hurling, tumbling
as rubble headlong into dark,
crammed into Wall to defend a fortress.

They lay estranged for fifteen centuries
till man turned tender, cradled them
one by one securely up into the light,
honoured each with a number,
deciphered their stories, stood them,
sheltered in a gallery, open to visitors'
view. But never to be touched.

White Lines on Blue Metal I

Phoenix:
Unites a Painters' Guild;
white-ashed wings, body
blued in Cheshire breeze.
Poised mid-Millennium, awaits
what fires of re-birth?

Traversings:…. To Promenade

Canal turns heel at southern shift of Wall
and I discern a sea-change in my stride:
gentled steps and breath, a sigh let fall

at twin-flagged paving's slow incline.
Wall drifts shallow under shawl of trees,
and bares its ankle to the field inside.

I pause beside the rails and savour peace
that havened space allows to explore
the wider frame. Some stroll at ease,

clustered like the seeds of sycamore
that rustle in a conversational breeze.
Others pace alone, absorbed in thought

amid the mazescape of their minds, or deep
in mobile-speak with those apart. I think
of those whose distance lies in years - troops

whose sweat once murked Walls' coping rank,
or perfumed ladies, draped in air-blue silks,
their hems and lungs above the low street stink.

In denim's duller hue I trace their walks.

Trees by the Eastward Wall

No urgent axe has hacked
to clear threatened ground
so here, steady and serene

they have outgrown Wall,
crowns towering high.
They stand in long time,

gaze down decades, infuse
whispers adrift on the air.
But year by year their roots

weave deeper still. Nourished
on loss and detritus, what knowing
do they draw from earth?

Fragments of old tools, letters?
Mulch of concealed bloodshed,
tang of dried secrets, tears?

Nearer the Cathedral
their boughs proffer sanctuary,
verdant in prayer.

What Edmond Halley Saw from the Walls in 1696

He looked skywards, naturally,
as he took the air, yet still the sudden
shower of rain surprised; gust
of gull-grey clouds, contoured soft
as his Mary's tumbling silks, poured
its constellation of silver drops that
splashed on stone to coin the City's lap.

Shelled in a niche along the Wall, he saw
an Iris bow the earth, swathe of seven hues
from Great Fire flame to indigo of ocean
coved beneath a fainter arc. He scanned
the quietening sky and gasped: Another curve,
triple rainbow rare as a soap-maker's son
turned mapper of stars and tides. He wept

with awe at how a myriad liquid spheres
could dance in trinity of ribboned light till
comet-swift, his mind pitched back
to calculate cause and re-occurrence,
dissect the glow of generous heaven
stoled over him unforeseen, in colours
spun at elements' and his eyes' conjunction.

Sighting from the Walls 1858

And so the great ship appeared in his mind's eye,
berthed along the North Wall.
Mr Musgrave, woodyard owner, saw it each day
on his walk to work, and wondered,
as he strode along the Walls,
just how big a forest it would take,
how many wood-cutters would be needed,
and how many planks required
to construct the deck.
And how much money his small business
could have earned by so doing.

Mr Musgrave professed a numerary fascination.
He knew the ship's length as exactly
six hundred and ninety-two feet.
He had paced it out, prow to stern,
Phoenix Tower to the Kaleyard –
half-way along, opposite the Cathedral.
The ship's five funnels,
like stove-pipe hats,
thumbed the sky in contempt
at the Cathedral tower's reach for God.
Six masts, named for the days of Creation,
rose even higher; Mr. Musgrave noted
the paddle-wheel's central position,
between Wednesday and Thursday.

The yardarms formed mighty crosses,
like skeletons along the skyline.
Some days Mr Musgrave could not discern
if the air was clouded with fog,
or shrouded by unfurled sails.
His head swirled with dreams
of sailing to the ends of the earth,
and all the mines of England

plundered of coal to stoke
the mighty vessel’s non-stop voyage.

Mr Musgrave grew accustomed
to a grey-sailed blankness in others’ eyes.
It was in the mason he commissioned
to inscribe the Wall and make
a solid record of the ship’s double iron hull.
The craftsman shrugged,
picked up the chisel.
He carved an anchor and ‘692F,’
as instructed.
He curved the 6 and 9 like ammonites,
so they lay like fossils on the coping,
even after the S S Great Eastern slid sideways
into water, dissolving into mist
as Mr Musgrave slept.

When Mr. Brunel's ship was launched in 1858

and water smoothed the slice of iron's passing, a mason
scored the Wall to mark hull's reach from Phoenix Tower
to Kaleyard: '692F', anchored and catalogued in stone;

another notch upon the City's belt that holds
incisions of years: Murengers' marks; sharpenings
of arrows; channels gouged on towers by tow-ropes

of stone-faced canal-men - the incidental cuts as raw
and deep as those intended. Surfaces urge an asserting
of self, as Centurions once inscribed the Wall

that slaves built, their foreheads stamped ' tax paid,'
and soldiers' hands tattooed to bind their labour.
Rock is chiselled, skin inked, our boundaries claimed

as tablets to engrave the names of child or lover, lay
out an identity in Celtic knot or dolphined ankle,
story the body with our art, our life, the icons of our faith.

All fade as ageing flesh must fray our neat designs.
Mr Musgrave's wonder lies as dust, the great ship scrapped,
its length, as weathered curiosity on stone, survives.

Shifts of Perspective

In 1855, John McGahey drew a detailed aerial picture
of Chester as seen from a tethered hot air balloon.

He had no idea how long he'd stood,
defended from gravity by a basket
under balloon-skin, to sketch
the city as only birds had ever seen,
its walls and streets veined like a leaf.

Later, others' eyes turned slant,
though they trilled at his depiction,
professed charm at the art of one
who looked down on them, measuring
their mansions with his finger-tips.

Yet now he too felt tiny, a stray husk
hollowed light on a granary floor,
as if the thread that tethered him
to earth might loosen and leave
him to float alone, beyond the Wall.

White Lines on Blue Metal II

Decorative Cross:
Grounding of faith.
Limbs blossom and curl
stark gallows into soft lifelines;
stir worship through centuries.
O Lord, open thou my lips.

Liturgy of the Hours

A voice, seedling-thin through dark air.
Domine labia mea aperies
Sunrise crumbles the night.
"Unlock the Kaleyards' gate,
that the King of glory may enter
and his servants go out in safety!"

Crenellated kale, feathered purslane
rustle, the breeze a harpist's stroke over
leaves ranked more orderly than Eden.
Through the little hours, rectangular beds
bulbed with onions, cream-green orbs
of fennel, rest under toiling hands.

The Black Monks murmur like bees hovering
round borage flowers; kneel to weed,
bow to dig. To work is to pray.
Dusk's cowl calls curfew and Vespers' shelter.
"Let the righteous enter his Gate with praise
and the oak be closed against marauding Welsh!"

They lie in cells, meditate in silence,
robes dark as soil, souls wrapt as chicory.
Outside, rigid-fingered skirrets and carrots
press into hard earth, hands of prayer
against the terrors of uprooting in the night.
Deus in adjutorium meum intende

Part 2: Eastgate to Bridgegate

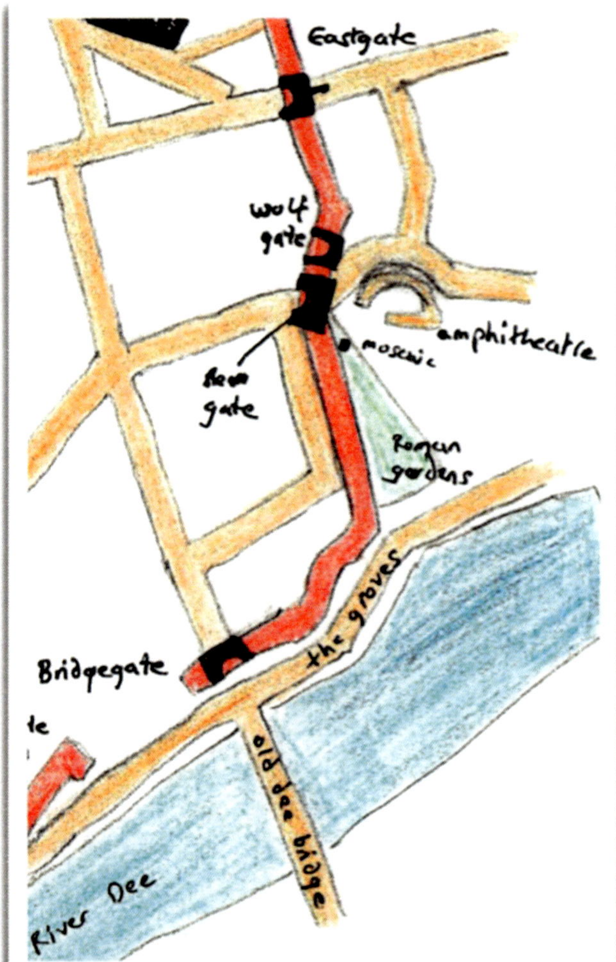

Perpetuum Mobile

'In two thousand years there has not been a single day without people walking this street below,'

says our guide. We stand on Eastgate
under the land's most-photographed clock,
stare down at the thronged, cobbled street:
Straight as a rod;
Kelsall to Wales;
Via Principalis.

Murmuring voices swell, bees rippling the breeze.
The human river flows, diverts by sudden jerks,
pedestrians parting as random taxis corner
into the current
to land the rich
at Grosvenor Hotel.

In disarray fit to shame a Roman soldier,
civilians stroll in clusters or alone, almost
uniformed in trousers, bags cross-bodied;
continue the footfall
unawares;
tread on ghosts.

I descend stone steps to enter the scene
at ground level, no spectator; forsake
the long view for this moment.
Now passers-by
may see me eye-to-eye.
But still don't.

White Lines on Blue Metal III

Eastgate Clock:
Roman-numeralled, gilded,
City's long-service watch
holds steady the hours; empowered
to halt steps of tourists, swiften
the time-pressed.

Fallen Angels

You look startled with your set lips,
brows frozen over apple cheeks.
Are you shocked to find yourselves here,
eight disembodied spirits, stationed in pairs
around a giant carriage clock
on the mantelpiece of Eastgate Wall?

Wrought iron and sandstone is a drop down
from heaven's crystal halls and the swords
of fire you held at Eden's gates.
Now all you guard is the Diamond date
of an earthly Empress' reign; in a fortress city
at peace, you chaperone time for all comers.

Do you brim with anger, crammed
into corners, your heads held rigid,
sprouting sky-blue wings for ears?
You could not hear nor stop the thieves
who came to steal the only hands in sight
on the clock-face, beneath your eyes.

Your vanity wings, trimmed with gold,
leave you pinioned on a box built
to house a hundredweight of pendulum,
aching your brains with the throb of time.
Eternal creatures, forced against each second
of the Walls' passing hours.

Your annunciation tamed into decoration,
you become extras in a thousand images
of beaming Japanese or gawky teenagers.
Cherubs afloat above iron curls, brick-red roses,
you have endured over a century,
watching us walk under time's shadow.

Snapshot

‘Will you take our photo, please, under this clock?’
Two willowy girls, hair flowing like a fairy-tale,
hail me with smiles and i-phones atop Eastgate.

They’re Liverpool students, final term; first time in Chester;
They’re loving these old buildings;
They've just been into the *cutest* branch of Superdrug.
‘It’s how people imagine England to be,’ says the chestnut-tressed.
They’d no idea that Chester has Walls.
Nor that they are standing on them.
‘Amazing,’ says the flaxen-haired, wide- eyed.
‘We thought this was just a little bridge.’

I wonder what they hope to graduate in,
point along the paving, my arms spread wide
like an air hostess demonstrating safety procedures.
I suggest they head towards the river.
‘Will we find a café?’ Refreshments, I assure them,
will be available. They can walk on to the race-course.
‘Oh, yes,’ Chestnut nudges Flaxen, ‘I’ve heard of that.’
By now, I can’t help myself. I tell them

How the Romans first built the Walls;
How this is the very entrance to their fortress;
How the Walls have repelled Vikings, endured siege, but
this is becoming a lecture they never signed in for.
I take Flaxen’s i-phone in its bridal-white case,
the screen ice-spidered with cracks.
‘Look for the Walls maps to check where you are.’
I sound like an anxious mother hen.

I hold the i-phone aloft. The screen looks blurry.
'Perhaps you have your thumb over the lens?’
She teaches me gently, patient with my ignorance.

Traversings: Blurred Edges

Past Eastgate
an upthrust of brick quilts the skyline;
buildings' backsides moon at Wall,
who throws in the towel, turns
pseudo-street between roof and ground.

Nothing matches.   All
At
                Odds.

Brick: terracotta to weathered-black.
Wall.
Concrete: jaded multi car-park grey.

He says *he likes* this place
when we walk here -
its Amongstness.

Windows at right-angles to Wall
                  or face-on and blank
                            or half-drooped with a single curtain.
Everything trimmed with metal as
                  spikes string windows and roofs and
                            railings line the walkway to

make Wall outsider
within City sprawl
no neat divider

A lilac sapling pushes from a roof-edge,
roots forcing bricks below out of kilter.

of these insistent occupants of space.

Cheek by Jowl

Out the back he only saw what he sought:
Cubed red Biffa bins, huddled as smokers askew
by the yard wall. He tipped trash into their yaw,
deposited another silver beer barrel
onto a cluster that massed like fish-spawn.

Mornings he mapped the gaps, his eyes
trained on each inch, angling his car into dock,
a held breath away from a paintwork graze.

Otherwise he didn't loiter in the stale
squeeze of air in this dank stone hold,
bounded by the lour of ancient Wall;
shrugged off the pocketing of his world
as just another bloody wall, after all.

Walls by Oddments

The Saxons defended Chester with bees and beer: They poured boiling ale over the Walls and scattered the town's beehives over their Viking attackers.

A statue of Queen Anne from Chester's old Exchange building once stood by Bonewaldesthorne's Tower. It was taken from its alcove over fifty years ago and subsequently vanished without trace.

The Eastgate Clock was officially opened on Queen Victoria's eightieth birthday, two years later than planned after her Diamond Jubilee, which it commemorates.

The Dee Bridge was the city's only river crossing into Wales till the Grosvenor Bridge was built. Its seven arches are all of different dimensions.

Ships once unloaded cargo at Shipgate, along the south Wall. Shipgate was removed in the Nineteenth Century and now stands in Grosvenor Park.

The Wishing Steps were created when the Walls were levelled into promenades. It is said that if you run all the way up, down and up the steps again without taking a breath, whatever you wish will be granted.

Kaleyard Gate was constructed to give the Benedictine monks easier access to their vegetable gardens. Chester Cathedral keeps its curfew by locking the gate each night.

Chester Racecourse was once a tidal pool of the River Dee. The west Wall incorporates parts of the Roman harbour Wall. In the Middle Ages, Watergate was the main landing point of a busy sea port.

In Tudor times, the daughter of the Mayor, Rauff Aldersey, escaped through Wolf Gate (also called Pepper Gate because of the nearby spice trade), to elope with a young draper. They fled to Wales.

Elopement to Wales, 1573

The night is breezed with cinnamon and clove -
grains that slipped their traders' hands to drift
beyond the Walls. A shadow sighs: her love
awaits, his thick-maned horses flick
their heads, and reins bunch knuckles hard
as a Mayor's grip constrained his precious girl,
set in stone, her whitened finger ringed
for a grey-lipped worthy's marriage stall.
This night the archway scrapes her breast; she edges
through to open sky, her lover's breath,
an urgent ride, to lie on sedge, be drenched
in spice and mist that dews them as they rest.
The father crushes nutmeg with his boot:
'The daughter is stolen! Lock the Pepper Gate!'

White Lines on Blue Metal IV

Roman Helmet and Sword:
floats faceless, alone; stark
reminder of Deva Victrix.
Below, a costumed Roman soldier
shepherds children two-by-two
across the road.

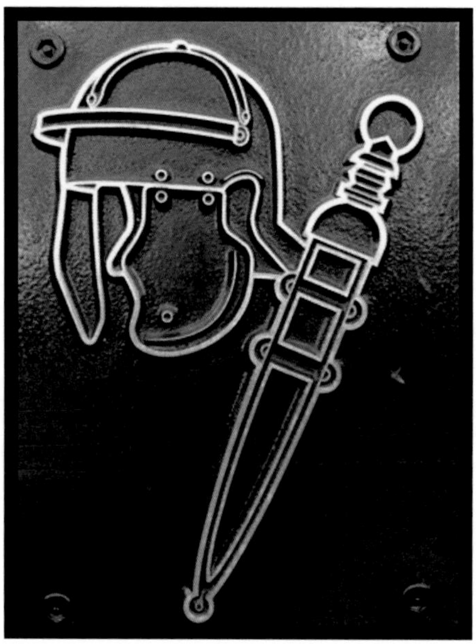

Traversings: On the Line

The relentless geometry of Conquerors
dissects continents into grids of red lines.
But here, by Wolfgate, Wall's kink defies
neat compass points to whisper a shift
of current: a vista of tree-rich sky
above an amphitheatre that sings
a football's bounce between two boys.

Onwards, and sun silhouettes the paving,
shades leafy boughs across its squares.
Creators divide - dark from light, air
from earth, stone from quarry - to shape.
Wall's spining towards the river splits
windowed office-workers, a dentist's,
from strollers round the Roman garden.

This is Wallest of Wall, a double-sided
drop that separates one space from another,
while lining up the disparate as neighbours.
My way on set in stone, I can look aside
at a boat's slow arc across the river's glitter,
or doors that hint at walls within the Wall.
Clear-eyed, I tread the seaming of worlds.

'So farre hath the God of heaven humbled this famous cittie'

Randle Holme III, royalist Alderman's son, on the Siege of Chester, 1645-46

You can staunch a Wall with anything
if you have to. Grab whatever; fling
hard and high with wool packs;
wrestle feather beds to straddle a gap
six horsemen wide. Scant sleep
to be had now as cannons pound night
into day, grind every edge. The King

bolts like quarried deer; a church
is sanctuary to culverin; fighters
for the orange sash or crimson,
blaze and roar like homes torched
to lay Roundheads bare. Streets
jostle with billeted soldiers, flint-eyed;
Clutching hands grime fresh coins.
This city has surrendered her silver.

Any dreams snatched are breached
by figures amok on the Walls;
the breath of falling bodies shrieks
of brandy and gunpowder, mingles
with a stink of musket smoke
and fetid dung that plugs the Eastgate.
Stomachs are shrunk raw, chewing

on promises of relief. Citizens pray
the Walls will hold, awake in beds
that buttress stone, scalps chafing
on obstinate ground. Dawn crusts
the sky; they wonder what granadoes
have hurled down in the night;
how their world will stand if Walls fall.
And what it would be like to eat a rat.

The Night the Walls came down

They took down the Walls overnight.
Tour Guides moped into pints at the Bear and Billet, amid
dark mutterings of 'Health and Safety gone mad.'
Jericho sent a condolence card whilst York looked smug.

They took down the Walls overnight.
Car-drivers sensed *something different* - the light,
pedestrians massed to cross the road - but couldn't say what.
The City felt as if the teeth had been pulled from its mouth.

They took down the Walls overnight.
Chester wobbled on its sandstone plate, a blancmange
set on gateau'd layers of centuries' old trash.
Back yards lost their back but gawped at new neighbours.

They took down the Walls overnight.
The Council saved a half million on repairs, then rowed
over how to spend it; the cost of old photos rocketed on e-bay.
No-one could watch the Races for free from Nuns Road.

They took down the Walls overnight.
Youths found the Eastgate clock dumped in the Kale Yard,
ran amok with it all over the Dean's field.
Locals who'd 'always meant to do the Walls ' felt cheated.

They took down the Walls overnight,
Folk-singers crooned laments and poets wrote elegies;
The media made documentaries and lovers rekindled memories.
The ghosts of Castra Deva were loosed, a wailing lost legion.

They took down the Walls overnight,
Businesses would sue, but did not know whom to blame.
Some said the Council, others aliens, that the street artist famed
for painting Daleks on the Eastgate was a prophet.

They took down the Walls overnight.
Heritage groups pressed for restoration;
Planners said no, build new ones, update them.
Others shrugged, said you get used to anything in time.

The Wishing Steps

Run upsteps, downsteps, back upsteps again.
My dearest wish will come to pass if I
draw no fresh breath until I reach the end.

I wish my share portfolio would rise;
I wish that all my bills were half the size.
Run upsteps, downsteps, back upsteps again.

I wish that I could tell her how I feel;
I wish that I could think before I spiel.
Draw no fresh breath until you reach the end.

I wish I could regain my youthful glow;
I wish I was eighteen and leaving home.
Run upsteps, downsteps, back upsteps again.

I wish, oh how I wish to be a Mum;
I wish my son would give up playing the drum.
Draw no fresh breath until you reach the end.

I wish that she would leave that man for me;
I wish he would propose on bended knee.
Run upsteps, downsteps, back upsteps again.
Draw no fresh breath until you reach the end.

Sonnet of the South East Aspect

This stretch of Wall is not a factoried prose
of bricks spat out in rows, but eloquence
of ashlar; hewn from common rock, each stone
uniquely honed and placed to form this dense
dividing block. We could dissect these lines
to chart the salt erosion, contour scaling,
the layering of later colours – grime
and green of algae, lichen's sallow blotching.
But come, approach this artwork open-faced.
Expose your skin to ruddied sandstone, roughed
by rain and bone-grey flecked, now trace
the chill that films across your fingers. Above,
a myriad islands swell in moats of mortar,
and high in cove-worn stone a pigeon shelters.

A Dandy Escorts his Beloved by the River Dee, 1787

My dear, your winsome smile has so disarmed
all will and wit to stand against your charms.
So let us promenade beneath the Walls,
along the tree-lined Groves, and cause
admiring eyes to turn with envious passion
at such display of slender-figured fashion,
like Bridgegate's new simplicity of line.
Oh, Mr Turner's delicate design!
Its elegant arch ensures no Welsh incursion,
exquisiteness of taste being their aversion.

Where soldiers – Roman, Royalist, *coarse,*
patrolled these Walls, in pompous milit'ry force,
this nobility of structure now supports
our weightier walks of social intercourse.
Ascending the Recorder's steps, displays
your coloured stockings' stripes, the season's craze!
Fairest, do not scuff your coat, so graced
and keenly fitted to your shapely waist.
Your snowy ruffle gleams 'gainst rusty parapet,
that cannot boast your daily hour's toilette.

Surveying the river's aspect we'll take pleasure
in boldly claiming Chester as a treasure,
then drop our gaze with studied inattention
to glance at those below with condescension.
We'll seek to spy Earl Grosvenor on his stroll,
then saunter on to Eastgate's Royal Hotel,
luxuriate in company and dance,
partake of coffee, win at cards perchance.
For I'm smitten by your dazzling reflection
in this mirror, champagne-polished to perfection.

White Lines on Blue Metal V

Fortified Gateway:
Two towers frogmarch a portcullis,
Thick-set doormen, lost
to an arch admitting all
from the other side - the clubbers,
the charioted in their vintage tour bus.

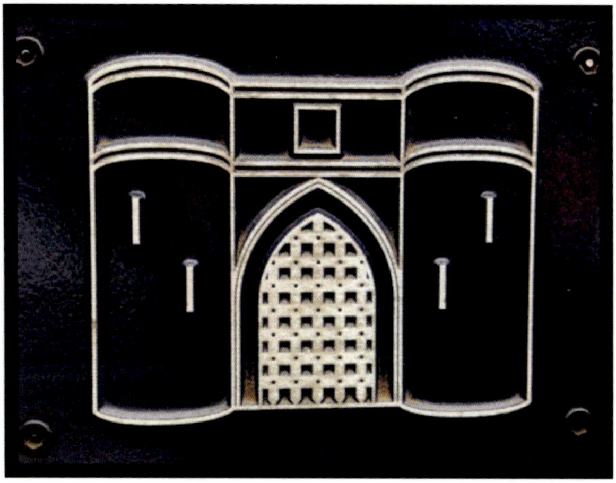

Bridgegate

Walls may be strengthened with silence, rock
or severed heads along a river's bank,
as watch is kept on chill stone towers.

Welsh vengeance floods to fire, torches all
to Tre-Boeth: burnt town. Wind whirls
high with ash and English soldiers curse.

Dafydd dead and Edward's law imposed,
the traders come in droves through 'Welshgate,'
pouring in like water pumped uphill.

The hill-grazed sheep are skinned to clothe
the City; grates are filled with Flintshire coal.
They claim Welsh boasts ring louder
than their swords, but call on them in war
when Englishmen besiege the City Walls.

Peace. The shattered Gate rebuilt as arch
admits each one in this United Kingdom. Still
Llywelyn's sons must mind their place: partake

of tea and scones; be told they must not meet
as more than three lest spirits stir in song;
be teased about the ancient crossbow threat

to Welsh within the Walls when sun has set.
They forget: Caerleon was under sway of Powys.
That bloodied line of heads stared with their eyes.

Interlude

Traversings

And so it comes to this, down from Bridgegate
onto level road as Wall seems to disperse,
sprawl flat as an oil spill: The *'almost*

complete circuit' the tourist guide foretold.
My steps drag like coal sacks in dismay.
What to do when waters flow delta-wide,
or trails peter out in the heart of the forest?

Like a ring removed, redundancy served,
planned children turned ghost:
the loss of an assumed future.

Absence of bearings halts many,
begets wanderers. What remains
but to walk on in unknowing, trust
to form beyond silence? I pass

a building where high windows watch
the hidden river, press towards Wall's rising
and the whisper: 'This is the way, walk in it.'

Part 3: Bridgegate to Watergate

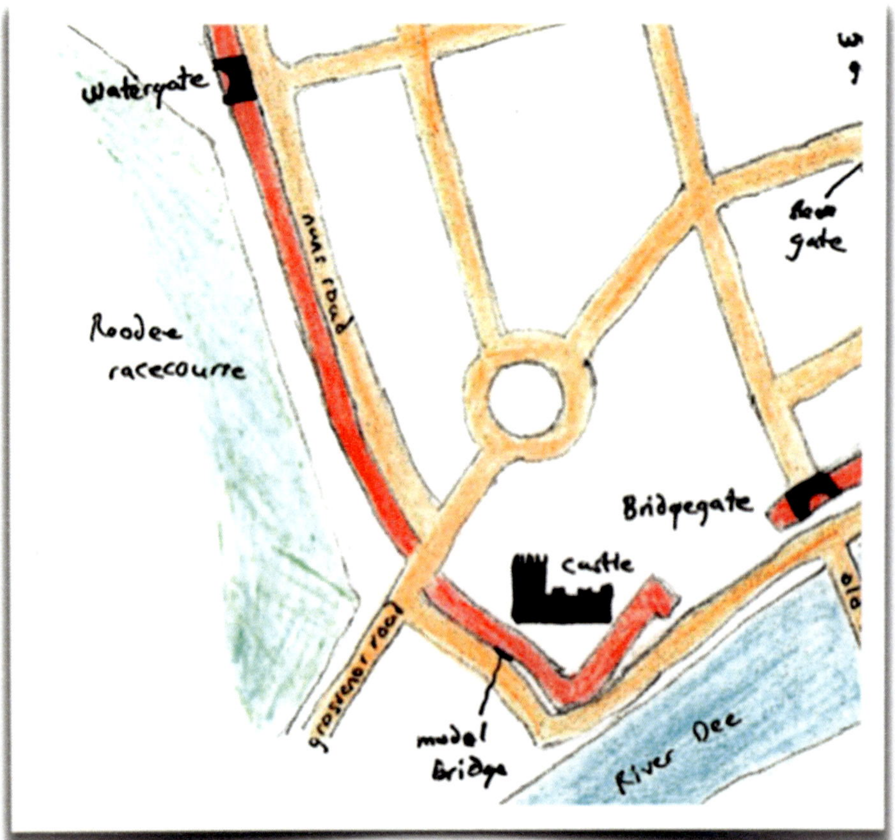

Ship Gate

The hole in the Wall was not cast aside
but borne, piece by piece, to the Park,
a stone's throw away, and re-assembled
as breath held across a path.

Its grainy sandstone frame, braced
against weight of sky, rainbows
an open space that lacks the gate
to separate ship from city.

Scabbed over with slabs, the Wall
is unsettled as are all torn places
when mended. Gaps, transplanted
to discreet glades, lace through lives.

They seep memories, mapped by scars,
wince under strangers' stumblings,
are anointed by their listenings. Spaces
honoured, enfleshed alike by sun and rain.

Traversings: Under the Eye of the Castle

Perhaps it's my Saxon blood that stirs
as I round the south-west Wall,
emerging in the Castle's lee: I shudder
at this stone-faced Norman thug
astride the motte. He stands
as if with ruddied, folded arms,
lords it over open air. I am pygmied.

On Boxing Day we walked these Walls.
Ice-crystals glistened under a thin sun.
We gripped the fence for fear our legs
would lock like starfish splayed on paving.
I swear the Castle sneered down
through narrowed eye-slits.

It's just a front. Behind, the Georgian
postscript rises: ample palatine
at ease in holding Court. Cars
line up below as tight as chain-mail.
Past Castle's stare I reach the road
that crosses Wall; wait; grip keys
in my pocket till the metal warms.

Hugh, first Norman Earl of Chester

Rings meant nothing: he bedded whom he willed;
plundered the flesh of forests, tore
quarried meat with teeth to feast his fill.
Now his belt pulls, stomach a mill-stone
wheezed towards Calvary; garters' lacing
chafing his legs to raw red lattice.

He ruled remote and mighty on the motte,
his Castle bailey, sanctuary of power;
glared down with curling lip upon the harried.
Tired eyes like mist-glazed jewels dart
as passing Saxons catapult their sneers:
'There goes Hugh Le Gras, The Fat.'

The river's arm could not corral his lust.
Hugh Lupus stormed the dragon's land,
a Wolf ablaze to Wales' Western shore.
His Abbot's tonsure palisades a quiet mind,
his own, nightmared with corpses, the cries
of dying infants so sharp he claws his bed.

Hugh D'Avranches rained coins for monks
to build upon a flood of gold; dammed
the river's flow to bless their mills with water.
Hungry now for God's embrace, he yields
to bind of holy vows. Let others Wall
the City round; his days are ringed.

Little Job

Fearing the crash of limestone into water
and a spate of shaming headlines
they said ‘Build small.
Show us a model of how it will be.’

So he made this tiny bridge, six-foot link
to nowhere, nestling in the grassy bank
below the City Walls, its modest span
a proof the bigger job would stand.

Robed in white, a blue-eyed teenage girl named
the edifice that bore her royal weight:
Grosvenor Bridge, carrier of Britain’s glory;
the largest single stone arch in the world

for thirty years, till greater spans surpassed
its boast, the silting river’s swell reduced
the sail-high gap and Victoria, crowned Queen,
forgot those little early jobs.

Properties of New Red Sandstone

'One of the first things you notice about the Walls is their distinctive red colour.'

The Cheshire basin contains rich red sandstone layers up to 1100 metres thick.

New Red Sandstone consists almost entirely of quartz grains, cemented together with the ferric iron oxide Haematite, giving the rock its red colour.

In the Triassic period 250 million years ago, sandstone was formed in a tropical desert of burning sands. Plate tectonics pushed it towards Britain.

Around 12,000BC, the Ice Age ended. Receding glaciers and ice sheets exposed valleys, lakes and plateaus.

Deva was built on a hill, the River Dee skirting round it in a gorge. The Romans quarried sandstone from the river's cliff outcrops for their fortress.

In AD 87, the Romans refurbished the Walls. The Earthen rampart front was cut back, creating a vertical face, on which the sandstone was set.

Slaves and criminals did much of the hard labour, levering, hammering and splitting the stone.

Sandstone is not uniform; stones are chosen carefully. The indentations on some individual stones are masons' marks.

The original Roman Wall was built of pebbly red sandstone. Medieval building and later additions were fine-grained red sandstone.

Traversings: Set Apart

No Nuns along Nuns Road, no Black Friars nor grey-habited
Franciscans, just a bunch of suits drinking outside The Architect

on land that once held sway from barracks down to quay, its soil
expansive host to small-holdings and souls.

Now no sailors shout beyond the Wall, but race-course,
bowling green, tennis courts instead mark space for sports;

lines laser-sharp, grass gleaming even emerald - and empty.
This side of Wall, time drifted ground downhill to make it

road-level, form a balconied dress-circle for a matinee
cancelled today. I look for where community may be:

the school for girls or old Infirmary - pioneer of quarantine?
Their windows stare me out cold, blank the sun's stream.

I am brushed by wistfulness, soft as August leaf, its green
tinged with dust, dry of Spring's sap. Space to learn or heal,

pray or play in company has seasons too. This hour is fallow.
I hear my steps turn slow. In solitude my footfall mellows.

Invasion

Their horsemen speed the field like torpedos.
Hooves pound past the Wall; flanks ripple
under whips of hunched silks. The army sprawls
the plain. Officers lounge round white pavilions
or rest in tiers under terracotta tiles;
rank and file throng tarmac or sit on grass.

The men: dark-legged and light-shirted;
The womenfolk: gaudy as parrots, stemmed
on stilettos or freighted with platform heels.
They line up by red-lit black tablets or weave
through crowds with vessels of amber liquid,
punnets of grease-gold snacks. At sundown

they surge through Watergate to pour uphill,
sobriety's shield askew. Discarded bottles
scatter the streets with emerald shards
as scuffles plunder citizens of their sleep.
Disarmed by lager and their own shots

they stagger in well-worn retreat. At dawn
they call chariots and pay their way home.
The City fills its bins, tallies its tills.

White Lines on Blue Metal V1

Two Butts Spill Eleven Fish:
herring, perhaps, or salmon
from Ireland - dearer.
Token of tonnage landed
too early, by centuries,
to be served up with chips.

Homage to Watergate

To this gate under St Peter's eye I bring
a heap of staring salmon. Let their wet stink
mingle with two butts of herring, red smoked
and white salted, a piquant army, brine-soaked.

At this riverless entrance I open
a tun of red Gascon wine, its aroma
rich-peppered with clove and ripe berries,
and tang of green apple with sweet pear.

Where stone reflects sundown I leave
a swathe of linen from Ireland's leas,
buttermilk-steeped, soft-water rinsed,
aired in bright meadows where butterflies dance.

At the base of this arch I set
Anglesey limestone, soaked with the sweat
of carriers and merchants' shock at so many shillings
to ship ocean-aired stone for corn millings.

Under this plainest of gates I offer
armfuls of pelts, still reeking with fear.
Squirrel, marten and deer, stiff with the smell
of dried blood, destined as a tanner's haul.

Let the Wall breathe in all to remember the days
when Watergate seethed with the haggling of trade,
with cargo and commerce, the life of a port
betrayed as the Dee diverted its course.

And what if our enemies threw flowers,

lassooed us in daisy chains, flung bouquets
that hazed rose-scent over toxic proposals?
Or simply let birds and breeze carry seed
over a wall to lodge in cracks behind the lines.

See here by the Watergate,
how clusters of purple stars foam
and feather the sandstone face, charm
gritty edges, even as roots loosen mortar.

Hard-hatted and daygloed, a unit of three
counter the attack. One is dropped
in a harness down the Wall to extract
those velvet-petalled threats to defences.

Ripped from their holding, tossed onto paving,
discarded blooms lie like limp bodies
that fell – or jumped – from the City Wall.

On Reading the Murengers' Rolls of 1441

How can I read these unravelling rolls, silent as Walls?
I weight the stranded scrolls, layered like leek-skins,
as strips of young cream interleave ancient paper,
mottled grey and dun as fox-hide, fawn-pelt,
grain-soft as fur with a tang of drying bracken.
Black ink faded to mushroom columns the surface,
balanced tidily as piled stones in four-line blocks.
The scribe casts each line with a fish-hook stroke.
No fish are caught in this murky water, but see how
this murenger has repaired his down-sliding hand,
laddering his roll with rungs to steady thick-set script:
records of tolls, merchants and masons charged;
an ordinary list to save the Walls from loosening stones;
a work of art, lines laced with loops and arches;
an imprint on an undulating sea.

An imprint on an undulating sea;
a work of art, lines laced with loops and arches;
an ordinary list, to save the Walls from loosening stones;
records of tolls paid, merchants and masons charged.
Laddering his roll with rungs to steady thick-set script,
this murenger has repaired his downward sliding hand.
No fish are caught in this murky water, but see how
the scribe casts each line with a fish-hook stroke,
balanced tidily as piled stones in four-line blocks.
Black ink faded to mushroom columns the surface,
grain-soft as fur with a tang of drying bracken,
mottled grey and dun as fox-hide, fawn-pelt,
as strips of young cream interleave ancient paper.
I weight the stranded scrolls, layered like leek-skins.
How can I read these unravelling rolls, silent as Walls?

Part 4: Watergate to Northgate

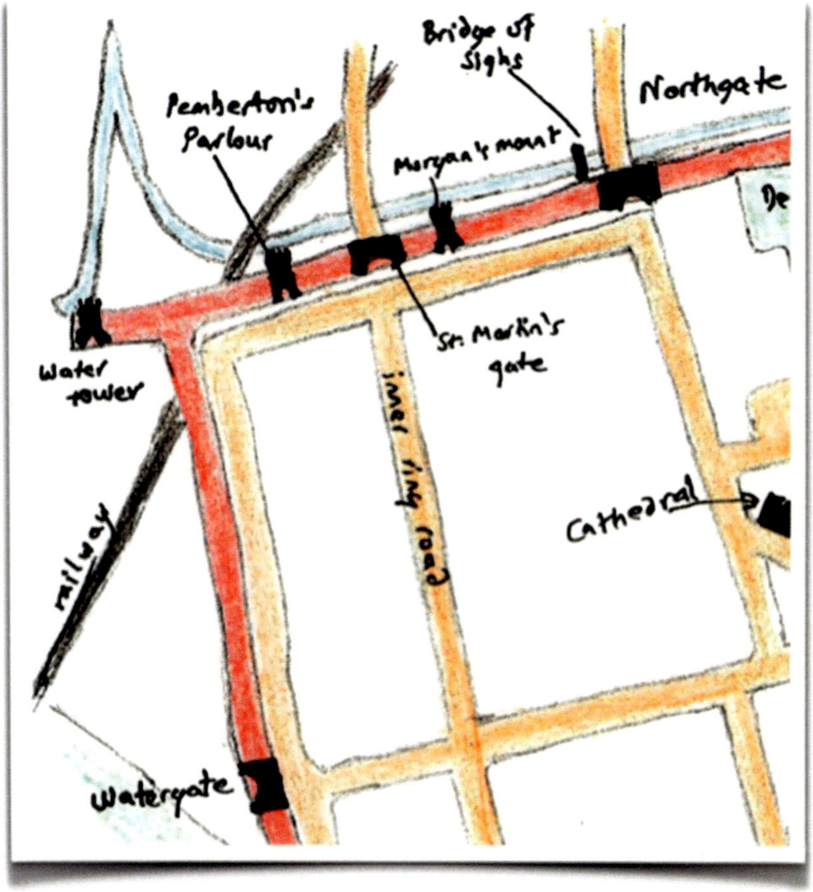

Traversings: Turning Point

A sudden punching whoosh and scrape slices
my thoughts: a train pierces the Walls twice,
clips this corner above a rising *basso continuo*
of cars that chase along surrounding roads.

In the Gardens red, white and blue trails
loop like ribbons towards the heart of a Maze;
Above, a piecemeal layering of Wall
cut by railway crossed over road bridging Canal;

deepest course the slowest, though direction is all.
Now I must turn at the tower, angling east
to interweave my way with others' journeys.
Dislodged from thoughts towards the City's noise

I wonder where true centre lies, and if all
our walking to and fro is quest for the elusive poise
between the innerness and outerness of things.
On the Canal, an empty plastic bottle floats.

White Lines on Blue Metal V11

Merchant Ship:
metal-flat sails becalmed
on windless azure;
safe above gardens suspended;
forever unharboured, mocked
by trains' passing roar.

The Wisdom of the Water Tower

1.Know your worth:
Brought into being at cost,
your value soon outpaces a price
of even a hundred pounds multiplied.

2. Do not envy Wall-tucked towers:
An outrider's eyes angle as no other.
Your kite-string spur of stone still
connects the genuine seeker.

3. Anchor the voyage-worn.
When sodden ropes threaten to wrench
the iron rings from your body, staunch
sailors' curses with twelve-foot thick skin.

4. Let them stare.
Remain unmoved by the resentful or the awed.
Artefact, matter-of-fact, however viewed,
most see not as you but as they are.

5. Never resist the drift of Autumn.
Receding tides lay bare the raw earth
that can seed-bed a garden; Death,
the herald of a different season.

6. Allow the curious inside
to scrutinise your beam-boned ceilings,
butter-milk walls with their sky's needlings.
Shared air need not steal lungs.

7. Keep your counsel.
There were merchants who cheated their tuns,
miscreants who kidnapped a stone queen.
Not all that is witnessed must be told.

8. Celebrate angularity.
We bear many faces, though few dare hold
their every rough edge exposed to the world
in all weathers.

The Men Who Know

The Men Who Know will tell you how it is.
They have kept vigil with musty books,
strained over water-stained documents.
Paid academics may have their opinions
on where Saxons settled or what Normans did,
but the Men Who Know will know.

The Men Who Know like to tell,
declaim *fortissimo* or assured *sotto voce*.
They will answer all your questions
and more, so do not ask
unless your dinner is in the slow cooker
and someone else will look in on the dog.

The Men Who Know have beards, wear
earth-toned sweaters patterned in geometric shapes.
They are on a mission
to convince Those Who Think They Know,
that things are otherwise,
rejoicing when a so-called expert concedes defeat.

The Men Who Know know more than
The Men Who Are Supposed To Know know.
And they know it.

The Men Who Know
see clearly how town planners should proceed
and where things have gone wrong.
With them in charge that Mall would not be standing,
and funds would flow for upkeep of ancient Walls.
It distresses them when towers are wrongly labelled.

The Men Who Know do not ache for fame or fortune,
just modest recognition.
See how the facts ignite passion in their eyes,
these self-appointed guardians of our heritage!
We look to them because they care.
Because they are curious.

Aethelflaeda, Lady of the Mercians

She was born as prows of long-ships tore the strand,
and flaxen hanks of sea-worn warriors flashed
beneath the moon's milk-eye to beach on English land.

Alfred's girl, and quick to spurn the needle for the sword,
to brace the targe, ride arrow-swift, her mind honed sharp
in arts of weaving peace with tongue and blade.

First lady of the boundary-folk, she rebuilt Deva;
stretched its Walls to kiss the river's edge; secured
the Kingdom's hem from enemy invader.

Widowed by Danish blades, a Queen alone,
who long had shunned a husband's touch, fearing
the pain of a baby's birth and her body torn.

The Naming of Pemberton's Parlour

I read the panel: 'Pemberton's Parlour,'
on this scaffolded cove and wonder
if you mourn your wilder name.
A clock-turn could unwrap your pipes and planks;
remove the panel; allow the graven names
upon your yellowed plaque to sharpen
into prophecies of mayors and murengers.

A drift of smoke thickens to a snort
and metal clatter: the Railway Age.
Masons unmake you, and every train
shudders your joints as sandstone grains
nuzzle your sides to shape again.
Grime-faced navvies rip up track, unhole
the Walls; buildings dissolve into a grove.

Below, men make a rope-walk, trudge
to and fro unstranding chains of flax.
Among the overseers of unravelling
with tricorn hat and cane: Pemberton.
His multi-buttoned coat and breeches
warm your gazebo seat; fit,
he says, for the Queen herself till

you are dismantled, half-moon body
torn to rounded base, a crumbled ruin.
Folk grow haggard; King's Men surge
and shoot; Cannon balls press the rubble
of your wounds, then swoop up to sky;
scattered ashlar swarms, fills your fractures.
You tower twice as high.

Fulsome now you span the Wall, host
to watchmen's sweat and scanning west
towards the hills. The reddening sunset
blooms your stone with youth.
You stand strong at the edge of woods
where nameless shadows prowl:
Goblin Tower.

Walls by Adjustments

During the Civil War's Siege of Chester, cannons made two breaches in the Walls, one by Newgate and one between the Goblin and Water Towers.

In 1894, Pemberton's Parlour was re-built due to damage from train vibration.

Today the Walls are a Scheduled Ancient Monument, cared for by Chester City Council and English Heritage.

In 907AD, Queen Aethelflaeda strengthened Saxon defences by making Chester a key fortified town and extending the line of the south and west walls.

From 1307 to 1835, the Walls' repair was the responsibility of two elected officers called Murengers. They raised taxes or murage on goods entering the city to fund the masons' work.

Chester Castle was built by Hugh Lupus, first Norman earl, its wooden tower replaced by stone in the 12th century. After the Civil War it was extensively rebuilt along Classical lines. It has been used as prison, court, tax office and Mint.

There were once 22 towers round the Walls, built at a bow's shot apart.

When Newgate was added in 1938, its designers were so keen for it to have **a** 'medieval feel' that they put mock arrow slits on *both* sides of the Wall.

25 metres of Wall by the Grosvenor Hotel collapsed through rainwater damage in 2008. Restoration used ancient stones in their original locations where possible.

The most recent Walls' breach was to accommodate the Inner Ring Road. St. Martin's Gate, built to preserve the Walls walk, was opened by Barbara Castle in April 1966, as the Moors Murder trials were being held at Chester Crown Court.

Breach

You could be forgiven for missing it, eyes
on the bumper in front as traffic-lights
cluster cars along the Ring Road towards
Law Courts, Castle, Race Course.
This concrete staple pins the carriage-way:
St. Martin's Gate.

The gap that glared as rubbled wound
when road broke through Wall is smoothed.
Framed with a so-called gate, it bears
the name of church and parish
crushed for a new 'simplicity and lightness'
of clean-lined stone.

It was a time for loosing the young:
Flower-children danced; World Cup gleamed;
the Beatles gave All Their Lovin.'
Tongues met new words - *Barclaycard, Polaris,*
Hindley. Rhodesia deserted Commonwealth.
Cathy was not coming home.

Cut ribbon opened this unshuttable gate
as a Chester jury listened to a voice on tape:
a dead girl begging to go back to her mother.
Today, bridged above the cars' thrum,
two walk hand-in-hand where Wall
hangs by a thread.

White Lines on Blue Metal V111

Cannon:
Metal beast of Civil War formed
to let fly human fury.
Outline of its predator's hump still
warns that poison runs deepest
in the fire of friends.

Traversings: Full Circle

A sculptured cannon holds fire, frozen as iron
perma-rust below Morgan's Mount. I see Morgan,
smoke-stained, eyes glazed with shock
at Wall he defended, bulldozed for a road’s sake.

Behind, Pemberton's Parlour, meshed in a nest
of metal. Crumbled joints await the masons' redress.
Beyond, Welsh hills endure as each generation
chooses what to mend; to break; to leave. I walk on.

Wall is corridored between high trees and street
where Victorian buildings revive Tudor gables. Uphill
I press, that familiar angle of steps that near an ending,
A lamp-post inks the Northgate skyline, once bulked

dark with a debtors’ prison, the legs of the hanged
dangling at its windows. I reach the summit, end
of journey unremarked by gate-top saunterers.
The air drifts with savours from a Tapas bar below.

Cars pass to judder old dungeons; discompose ghosts.
There are voices behind me on the steps:
“We've been right round now. Done the lot."
"Cathedral, then? Or a coffee shop?"

Writing on the Walls

town walled all aboute with battle ments and a walke all round pav'd with stone.
tortuous wall-girdle of the little swollen city wanders in narrow file between parapets.

four gates look on the
east to India,
west to Ireland,
north to Norway,

a marzipan slice of four coloured squares
bound with a thick rind - the stone that
surrounds

the city.
its arms round beautiful old Chester, while
ugly new Chester peeps over the parapet.

stone soft, reddish grit and friable, shining particles intermixt, apt to decay.

two may walk very commodiously side by side.

castle keeps and church spires
springing out of the wall in a clump
like flowers growing in a pot.
hemmed in, both inside and out, by houses.
on the other side, smoke and dust
and red-brick chimneys,

engineers carried out an assessment of the entire wall circuit... several areas were showing signs of movement...after a period of monitoring, propping was initiated at these locations.

views of huddled English town
and ordered English
country.

gave me only a much better idea of other
people's washing, gasworks
and the Canal.

Woman Dies After Falling from Chester City Walls

pear trees throw up
fruit-laden branches
to a level
with the parapet.

another cluster of those queer
little houses that cling to its top
like limpets.

old towers, picturesque and
overgrown with ivy
and wallflower,
peep out.

language of the stones bears a feeling of peace and soft melancholy.

convalescents, old persons, and delicate ladies come to breathe the pure air.
a ring road for walkers. Get on at any point, have a wander

Symbiosis

It's true, we were not birthed in love: Raised from earth
and come of age in stone to scorn your enemies'
wrath, left to ruin in wars' aftermath.

And yet, you did not turn your back when others tore
down city-clasping Walls, but soothed our face
from salt-air gnaw and cannon's smack. You shore

us still: stabilise, defoliate, mend our gritting gaps.
You pride yourselves our keepers, fit to walk
upon us as you choose: on urgent car park dash

or feted heritage trail. But we soak in your stories;
biographers, your lives inscribed in our sides;
unshifting anchors for your memories.

Northgate Revisited

I’d have expected more dross
on these stone flags, gleaming
with early rain - just a scatter
cigarette butts; lone beer bottle,
set upright; jam-sogged paper bag.
A ghosted wind has passed,
discarding old leaves that clump,
curled and sodden in crannies,
or lie spread-eagled under my tread.

Weeds green the Bridge of Sighs,
silenced walkway poised
high over the Canal, ending
at a bricked-up building.
Here, the City’s condemned
once faltered their way outside
the Wall under dry-eyed stares.
Today grass grows arrogant.

A man sweeps stray leaves
into a plastic sack, green as summer.
‘That looks like hard work,’ I say,
for want of anything better.
He narrows his eyes, brushes past.
Behind me my boot-prints
are etched wet on bare paving.
Under this crisp December sun
they will soon dry out.

Afterlude

Walls

Here by the Roman Garden gate, four seasons
depicted in mosaic: Handfuls of coloured stone
squares, cut and set, create a containing circle
of curve-limbed figures within wave-curling scrolls.

I look up at Walls' stones - gravel to the gods,
honed and heaved into straight defending line.
Even these stones not fixed, but restored
or replaced as years turn, changing Walls

to piecemeal anthology of all they contain.
This young mosaic too, a patchwork of scenes
of old Empire from Wiltshire to Constantinople.
We use what we have to create as we can.

I quarry the word-hoard, dapple pages piece
by piece with shapes. The Walls rise high,
endure long: a time-mosaic near two millennia
in the making. My words besides are fragments.

Chester City Walls

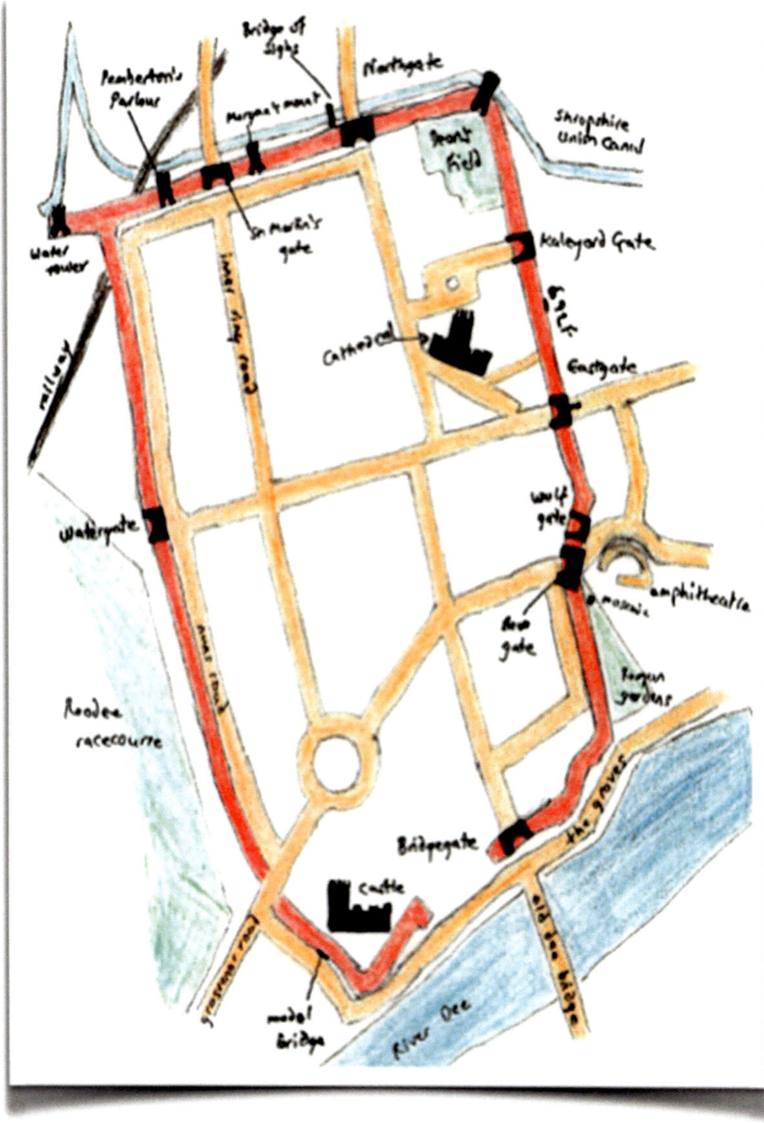

Acknowledgements

Pages 10,18,23,30,37,49,57,64 The White Lines on Blue Metal plaques can be found on interpretation panels positioned at key locations along the Walls in 2012.

P. 53 The photograph of the Murengers' Rolls for 1440-1441 is included by kind permission of the Chester Records Office.

P. 66 Quotations for **Writing on the Wall** were taken (in author order) from:

Celia Fiennes (*Travel Journals* c 1690)
Henry James (*The Ambassadors* 1903)
Lucian the Monk (*De Laude Cestri* 1195)
Garry Hogg (*Script for BBC Light Programme* broacdcast 1949);
H. V. Morton (*In Search of England* 1924)
Edmond Halley (*letter in Philosophical Transactions* c 1696)
Dr Samuel Johnson (*A Diary of a Journey into Wales in the Year 1774*)
T. H White (*The Once and Future King* 1958)
C. M. Kirkland (*US Boston Mirror 1848*)
New York Times (1881)
Chester West and Chester Council (*Walls Update* 2012)
Chester Chronicle (16th September 2011)
William Bigg (*Ten Days' Tourist* 1865)
Henri-Francois-Alphonse-Esquiros (*The English at Home* 1861)
Trip Advisor Reviewer (**www.tripadvisor.co.uk** accessed 2014).

I am indebted to the informative and illustrated website www.chesterwallsinfo, compiled by Steve Howe, and a valuable resource in researching the Walls' story.